The First Collection

Sarah Lipton-Sidibeh

T0349325

JACARANDA

TWENTY
in 2020
Black Writers, British Voices

This edition first published in Great Britain 2020
Jacaranda Books Art Music Ltd
27 Old Gloucester Street,
London WC1N 3AX
www.jacarandabooksartmusic.co.uk

A CIP catalogue record for this book is available from the British Library

ISBN: 9781913090173
eISBN: 9781913090371

Cover Design: Rodney Dive
Typeset by: Kamillah Brandes

Printed and bound by CPI Group (UK) Ltd, Croydon, CR0 4YY

About the Author

Sarah Lipton-Sidibeh BA Honours, LLCM, FRSA, was born in London, England. She has written short stories, poetry, a play, a children's book, film scripts, song lyrics and educational textbooks.

Sarah has written three volumes of short stories: *A Journey Into Fear And Fantasy*, *Psychological Tales* and *Crossing Time*. In the 1980s, Sarah's short stories, 'The Reincarnation' and 'The Ordeal' were broadcast on LBC Radio's 'Through The Night' programme. Sarah read a selection of her short stories and poetry on Resonance FM in September 2010 and on Omega Radio in March 2011. Sarah's short stories, 'The Sanctuary' and 'Femme Fatale' were published in the online magazine *Blood Moon Rising* in January and April 2012.

Sarah has written three volumes of poetry: *The First Collection*, *Poems: Social, Satirical And Political* and *The Seasons, Nature And The Environment*. Her poetry has been published in numerous anthologies. In the 1990s, Sarah received an award from The Poetry Society in England for some of her poetry. Also, she received commended and honours certificates for some of her poems at The Richmond Music Festival, England. Sarah's poem, 'Stagnation' was short listed in The National Anthology Poetry Competition in 2005. Her poem, 'Wishful Thinking,' was printed in 'The Poems In The Waiting Room' pamphlet in 2010. These pamphlets are distributed to hundreds of doctors' surgeries in Britain. Sarah was The Featured Poet in *Bareback Lit Magazine* in October 2012.

Sarah has written a play entitled, *Revenge*, a children's book called *The Spell*, film scripts and song lyrics. She was awarded a commended certificate for her song, 'I Wish,' from The United Kingdom Song writing Competition in 2016. Sarah has written two educational textbooks, *Beloved: A Critical Study* and *Understanding Lord Of The Flies*. She is completing her first novel, *14 Bensham Grove*.

Contents

The Seasons, Nature and the Environment

The Body

The Past

Bunta

You're one of the seraphs from Paradise,
Always so gentle, always so mild,
Friendly, graceful and full of good advice,
Never sad or with a temper wild.
Your heart has the warmth of the summer sun,
Your face is like that of the goddess of love,
Your smile is angelic, like a nun,
Your complexion as bright as the dove.

You are the rose surrounded by the thorn,
The pearl enveloped by the large sand dune,
From the snarling dogs you run like a fawn;
You're the surviving thrush twittering a tune.
Into this satanic world you were born,
A gift from hope that a new world's on the morn.

The World We Live In

Writing a Poem

What type of poem should I write today,
A lyric, a sonnet or an ode?
Should I write in rhyming couplets or blank verse,
Or should it be poetic prose?
But poetic prose doesn't sound like poetry,
So I think I'll avoid that style.
I don't want to be shackled by metre,
I want my mind to roam free
Without worrying about a fixed rhyme:
That 'bake' has to rhyme with 'steak,'
That 'run' has to rhyme with 'fun,'
It gets tedious all the time.
I'll avoid decasyllables,
I don't want to burden my brain,
I'll have some lines short and some lines long,
There's not a law that says this is wrong.
Shall I write in tercets or quatrains,
Septets or octaves?
I think I'll avoid the lot,
As these forms have been used so much.
Should I fill my poem with figures of speech?
Assonance and alliteration would be fine:
"Her starry eyes sparkled like a sapphire"...
Too hackneyed, I don't want to make them whine.
When I read the finished poem aloud,
I want my creation to make me feel proud.
What about simile or metaphor?
These can work well if original:
"Her hands were as gnarled as a tree's bark,"
"He was happy as a skylark"
I'll avoid the latter, it's too much of a cliché.

I'll replace it with a strong image:
"The trees were withered witches,
Battered by the wind,
Almost falling in the ditches."
I like that, it's evocative,
It paints a morbid picture.
It's symbolic of life,
Of how the weak are crushed by the strong,
Of how people are tormented if they don't belong.
Good, I have a title now,
I'll call it 'Life.'
I feel the theme as I write:
Man battling with life.
I've moulded my poem well,
I am pleased with myself.
It reads as if man's life is hell,
But I want it to have a strong ending,
So I'll use a rhyming couplet:

"Many are swallowed by the ditch,
Those that survive are the rich."

Land of Hope and Glory

Land of hope and glory,
She receives a welfare cheque,
Her reward for passing exams,
While opposite her bedsit
A homeless man shivers outside a shop door.

Land of hope and glory,
Squatters sit in derelict houses,
Eating bread and cans of beans,
While in the bed and breakfast down the road,
People are huddled in an infested room.

Land of hope and glory,
He's been on the waiting list for two years
To have an operation on his knee,
But he can't afford private health care.

Land of hope and glory,
The roads are clogged with cars,
There are diversions and roadworks everywhere,
Causing drivers another hellish day,
Lateness punished with a deduction in pay.

Land of hope and glory,
The pupils scream, the teacher yells,
When the bell rings she's attacked,
But no-one is expelled
Even though she was slashed with a knife,
Almost killed, a mother and wife.

Land of hope and glory,
They attack or steal for money,
To buy drugs to escape the everyday.
Some sell their bodies as this is a quick way
To get that income for their habit.

Land of hope and glory,
She sits on the throne proud and alone,
Sucking sixty million from the public purse
To feed her lavish life,
While outside another person commits suicide,
Does anyone care that he's died?

Trade Not Aid

Tony Blair declared:
"Africa is a scar on the world's conscience."
The continent is experiencing genocide
Caused by famine, war, HIV and AIDS.
The situation in Africa today,
Is that the economy is weak
Because its people are dying.
The ones surviving have been reduced to poverty
Because of the IMF and the European Union,
Which have forced Africa into debt,
And they have imposed unjust trade laws,
Designed to keep the continent poor.

Africa shouldn't have to plead
For welfare dependency.
Centuries ago there were powerful empires—
Mali, Senegambia, Songhay and Ghana—
Which became rich and strong through trade,
So the solution is not European aid,
But allowing Africa to establish
Its might of former days.

Colonialism blighted Africa's progression,
Its legacy has been regression,
Millions of its people were forced
To work on new world plantations.
Africa's greatest source of wealth was gone,
And this made the economies
Of Europe and America strong.

Today Europe gives Africa so much aid,
Guilt for its past wrongs.
If Europe wanted Africa to persevere,
It would allow her to trade with the West,
But Europe has a fear of this
As Africa would become strong.

Colonialism blighted Africa's progression,
Its legacy has been regression,
In the 1880s there was
"The Scramble For Africa"
When Europe colonised the continent,
Raping it of resources and making
Africans a subject people.
Africa became powerless,
While Europe saw it as
"The white man's burden."

Now Africa has so many wars,
So much political instability,
If its people aren't dying of
AIDS they're being shot,
European money is used for guns,
And Europe won't sell Africa cheap drugs,
So that its people can be saved.

Colonialism blighted Africa's progression,
Its legacy has been regression,
When the continent was carved up
In the nineteenth century,
Tribe was turned against tribe,
When African countries got independence,
A lack of unity caused political instability.

Europe must be forced to allow Africa to trade,
This is the only way the continent will progress.

Aid is welfare dependency,
And Africa doesn't want to be
"The white man's burden" in
The twenty-first century.

Oppression

The leech is sucking Wealth away,
And there's the electricity to pay,
I'll have to sacrifice a holiday.

The leech is sucking Wealth away,
I've been without food since yesterday,
I am feeling more and more ill,
All the money went on the gas bill.

The leech is sucking Wealth away,
I wanted to buy new shoes today,
But the rent is close to due
And my pay has yet to come through.

The leech is sucking Wealth away,
I had to take out a loan
Just to pay the bills on the phone

No holiday, no food, no shoes, just hell,
My home now resembling a prison cell,
The leech has sucked Wealth away,
And Poverty seems here to stay.

Cruelty

Little girl, why are you so evil?
Are you that unchangeable?
You must be because I've seen you kick, punch
And throw stones at the disabled girl
And when you hear her moan,
You laugh and call her names.
You certainly are capricious
Because from my window
I saw you the next day
With the same girl, playing games
As if nothing had happened.
She is so tolerant of you,
Patience is clearly her strongest virtue
But again you are up to your old tricks,
Deciding on a whim to begin hurling sticks,
And when she weeps you console her,
And then begin to play again.
The scene is always a temporarily happy one,
Because as soon as your friends appear, you run,
Ignoring the girl you've abused and befriended
In the same breath.
Your mother isn't upset by your behaviour,
Blinded from the truth of your ugly character,
Little girl, if you continue with your nasty ways,
You too will be abandoned by your friends one day.

Workaholic

He works a twelve-hour day
Because he has bills to pay.
His wife rarely sees him,
And he's a stranger to his children.
When he's not working he's asleep.
What benefits can he reap,
Apart from the money?

He hasn't had a night out in three years,
He's become like a lodger, so his wife fears
That soon the marriage will end.
He's unable to play with his children,
He has no hobbies and has lost all friends,
And he forgets important dates
Such as his wife's birthday.
This fills her with much dismay.

He's locked in a prison cell,
He's been put under a spell
As his life is crumbling before him:
His wife will become a divorcée,
His children will be orphans soon
Unless he can escape from bondage
And live rather than survive,
This is the goal for which he should strive.

Old Age

She sits alone in her cage,
Looking at television some days,
She peeps through the curtains now and then,
Watching people with their friends,
She wonders if she'll ever have human contact again,
Her books and her cat are her only friends.

Life battles outside her walls,
But he cannot break in and slay her
As the old soldier's sorrows have made her strong,
At a burglar she brandished a hammer,
She wonders what's gone wrong
With a society that has decayed,
She feels it's infested with worms,
And is plagued by dangerous germs.

She pulls the curtain across the window,
Puts on the lamp and decides to read,
She hears children outside cry
So switches on the radio to drown out the sound,
She hears drug addicts getting high
So puts on headphones and listens to Beethoven's Fifth,
Life can do her little harm.

Carnival

The streets of Notting Hill are bursting with people,
The throng swells each minute of the day,
They follow the floats with Calypso bands,
The music pulsates while the crowd gyrates,
They dance along Ladbroke Grove
Past sound systems whose basslines clash with Calypso beats.
Reggae booms and almost busts the ear drums,
As the revellers reach Portobello Road.

Sweat streams down the dancers' faces.
They are gasping for refreshment,
Buy canned drinks to cool themselves,
From stalls at the side of the road.
The procession continues to weave its way
Through West London on this August bank holiday.

Costumes of fuchsia, green and yellow sparkle,
Girls' faces shimmer with glitter,
Gold jewellery gleams in the sunlight,
Cameras click to record this event,
Which animates Notting Hill every year,
Making it the centre of Europe.

As night falls the streets still vibrate,
People groove to the music which blasts the air,
Some begin to make their way home
Passing stalls of curried goat and jerk pork.
Children smile with painted faces,
Whistles shrill out their own song,
A gang of girls cross the littered streets
To catch the last tube home,
And they will return next year,
When carnival will visit again.

Thirty Something

In your thirties you are sandwiched
Between youth and middle-age.
You have youth but wisdom too,
And your life is at a new stage:
You no longer feel a need
To go out every night,
And you don't need lots of friends.
What you once thought was a bore,
Such as theatre or cabaret,
You now find interesting,
And will want to stay,
Rather than get drunk at a pub or club.

It's not a crime to be single,
It's not like in the past,
But why marry, it doesn't last!
For a woman it was worse:
Over thirty and unwed meant spinsterhood,
People treated you with pity.
But why couldn't it be seen as something good?
At least you weren't a man's property,
Catering for just his needs,
Being devalued or controlled,
Trying to break the chains to be free,
To actually have a life,
And not just be a wife.

Now many women in their thirties
Have prestigious careers,
But while attaining equality
There looms the terrible fear
That if children haven't been born yet,
It's to their detriment,
As the biological clock ticks away,
And problems arise that the woman could prevent
If deciding to have a child by thirty-five;
Why does nature have to be this way?
It applies to a time when a woman's life
Was just marriage and childbirth.
This is not the case today,
A woman strives for more,
She doesn't want her life to be a bore.

Be Yourself

Girl, why do you wear a blonde wig?
And why do you wear contact lenses
To make your eyes green?
Don't you know that doesn't suit a black skin
And makes you look obscene?
Your brown eyes are beautiful
So why be ashamed?
Your black hair enhances your skin.

Girl, you've been looking at too many magazines,
They need to be thrown away,
Why do you feel you're only attractive
If you look a certain way?
Ignore what the beauty editors say
And be proud of your natural skin and natural hair.
You'll learn, beauty is many things
And you are one of them.

Posthumously

It seems that in death
Rather than life one is valued,
The years of struggle to achieve,
To be recognised for one's ability
Go unnoticed like a pin on the ground.
Riches that one should receive,
Often arrive far too late,
When one is lying in the grave,
Then praise suddenly abounds.
What was inferior becomes a treasure,
Perceived as "classic"
The work of a genius;
One's name transforms into gold,
And a life of pain could have been
One of pleasure.

The Arts

The arts colour the painting,
Making it bright and interesting,
Nuances of shade and light
Banish grey far away
To a place out of sight.

The painting develops
And civilisation is born
Out of the canvas.
Darkness is dead,
And a new age has dawned.

If the colours of the painting fade,
Ignorance will slay civilisation,
Darkness will resurrect itself,
And blindness to beauty will arise.

Five Minutes

Five minutes speed by like a cheetah
When life is lived in an interesting way,
Five minutes pass as slowly as a snail
When boredom has the time to strangle the day;
In a five-minute audition much can be done,
But five minutes of exercise isn't worth spit,
In five minutes flat a whole race can be won,
But it's too short a time to wash more than your pits.
A five-minute sleep doesn't nourish at all
But a five-minute dance can be thrilling,
In a five-minute speech much can be said,
But a five minute conversation is boring,
In five minutes someone who is very strong
Can prove it by lifting a lorry.
Five minutes is too short for a theatre show,
But endless when lost in the snow.
Five minutes is too short for a novel or play,
But fine for a poem or short story.
It's too short to stretch into a proper full day
But if you're dreaming, five minutes is plenty.

Stagnation

I am being swallowed by quicksand,
I am being suffocated with a plastic bag,
I am paralysed from the waist down,
By a ferocious ocean I'm being drowned,
I can't reach the top of the hill,
I am shackled to an iron pole,
I can't break free from the prison cell,
I am trapped down a dark, dank well,
My feet have been glued to the ground,
I keep falling off the galloping horse,
I have been buried alive,
And I know I won't survive.
I need to be able to climb the mountain,
Only then will my life begin.

Love and Relationships

Mother

You created, nurtured and loved me,
You guided me through each dark night,
Your kindness and devotion has made me see
Why I am happy, no longer in plight.
You are the diamond in an ocean of tar,
The single rose encased by the thorn,
In the bleak-black heaven you're a sparkling star,
The glowing sun that appears at dawn.
I shall always value and cherish you,
You shall always be part of my life,
I will be your clown when you are feeling blue,
I will protect you from evil and strife.
Mother, you are a seraph from paradise,
And like all saints you are without vice.

The Cross at Calvary

I look up at that face of pain,
At that stick nailed to a cross,
A stream of blood running down from that thorny crown,
Staining your forehead red.
In a moment you will be dead,
But you should not have suffered for mankind,
Wasted the wisdom of your teachings on the blind.

Your death is greeted by thunder and rain,
They lash at your body like the Romans' whip,
The sky is filled with sorrow,
Spreading darkness into tomorrow,
Extinguishing the light.

The cross has survived as a souvenir,
It symbolises your suffering under the Beast,
It reminds me of our mortal torment,
And of our unwillingness to repent.
Now sin unfolds its wings across the earth
We honour your death and remember your birth.

A Woman's Best Friend

When I awake I'm greeted by
Your beautiful face
You place your padded paw
In my hand and we shake.
You lick my face while I stroke your velvet coat,
Then up I get and brush my teeth
And you curl up on the bedsheets.

After breakfast we go for a walk in the park.
You trot by my side but soon decide
To chase a squirrel scampering by the lake.
A few minutes later you're my companion again,
But then you see your friend
And bound towards her barking happily;
You tumble and race, give chase,
Play bow, chase again—your usual game.
Soon your pal has to go but
You know you'll see her tomorrow.

The gloom of the afternoon brings rain,
So we return home again,
And lunch while watching films.
I sprawl on the sofa and you look at me
With those gleaming eyes.
To my surprise you pull off my socks,
Stroke my feet and I think how lucky
I am to have you, Sam.

Elimination

With the Tipp-Ex erase name after name,
Remove the phone numbers,
You'll never need them again!
When did he last call?
Last summer I think,
And then he didn't have much to say.

Shelley of Streatham,
She's the loyal dog one minute
But becomes a vulture swooping down on you
When everything goes wrong.
Forget her, she's a snake.

Why bother with him?
He's no good for you, that slim Jim.
So you went on a date,
That doesn't mean you have to have sex.
He's lucky he even got one date,
Considering he looks such a state!

You forgot to Tipp-Ex this one,
Old Jonathan, he wasn't much fun,
All he talked about was World War One,
You were always so polite to him,
I would have thrown his number in the bin.
You had nothing much to talk about,
And he would moan about his gout.

Gloria the gossip,
Wipe her away!
Your secrets were broadcast the next day,
If you see her, treat her like a stranger.

At last the book is blank,
A new life is beginning for you.
The rats have been cast to the drain.
Be cautious of new people you meet,
Never get to know them too well,
Because some day they could make your life hell!

Mikie

Those beautiful brown eyes gleam like pools,
Yet they express much sorrow and suffering,
That smile is as warm as the sun,
But it hides despair like a loaded gun.
You remain affable,
Killing pain with infectious laughter,
You are the sparkling star that never dims,
Even when life tries to steal your grins,
Your bear hug shows me your affection,
Your brilliant mind engrosses me,
You're an intellectual,
Adroit yet often exploited in work that you do,
You're a devoted father,
A son to be proud of.
That handsome face has been a magnet for women,
But not many have understood you,
Or been there to offer comfort that's steadfast and true.
You're an excellent lover, there's no other
Who can give me such great pleasure,
You've been my rainbow, my treasure,
I will cherish you forever.

That Woman

Our love was so strong we had a bond,
Which we thought couldn't break,
But a storm came and shattered that bond,
And I became a mistake.

I used to be your treasured gem,
But you now see me as a fool.
I used to be showered with affection,
But now you've turned so cruel.

As love weakened,
My life dimmed.
You stopped phoning and sending me texts,
I had become second best.

And why? Because that woman came along,
Your inspiration, your salvation,
She helped you cope when you were without hope,
Of escaping the lure of the bottle.

So now it's goodbye and this makes me cry,
As I treasure our happy memories,
The rainbow fades and life has become grey,
That woman has stolen the colours from me.

You've Gone Away

You've gone away,
And I feel a pain inside,
My heart feels like lead,
And I feel you have died.

You've gone away,
And so has the warmth of your smile,
Your tender touch, laughter and compassion,
Oh why couldn't you stay?

You've gone away,
And sunshine has been replaced by rain,
A black cloud hovers over my head,
And I feel I have been betrayed.

You've gone away,
Like a bird that's been freed from a cage,
To begin a new life far from me,
Oh why did you want to stray.

You've gone away,
And you might as well be in a grave.
My life has become bleak;
It's always January, never May.

Despair and Happiness

A wedding ring is life in a cell,
A wedding dress is a life of hell,
The blissful wife becomes the slave,
The nuclear family a shackle round the neck,
The mother is soon treated like an unloved dog.
The family fragments and a lover appears,
He nourishes the lily and
The years of sorrow soon disappear.
The wedding dress is packed away,
The single woman has replaced the wife.
The mother has become the prized jewel,
One life shed like a snake's skin,
Replaced by a fairytale,
Far removed from the prison cell.

The Seasons, Nature, and the Environment

Mad Weather

Spring, summer, autumn and winter
Seem to have disappeared.
The flies arrive in February
And everything feels so weird,
Animals have woken from hibernation,
Birds twitter in the trees,
Bees buzz from flower to flower,
This is so strange to me.
The temperature soars to 68°F,
The sun dazzles in a blue sky,
I have to wear summer clothes,
But in December? I don't know why.
January is like June,
June is like January,
There is snow in July now,
And sunshine in February.
There is no longer fog in November, just bright and sunny days,
There is never snow for Christmas,
Oh I wish I was far away!
In 1987, the gusts came in October,
Rather than in March;
A lack of rain in winter
Has left the landscape parched.
I long to go to a country,
Where the seasons have remained,
Where there's snow in winter and sunshine in summer,
As I really don't like change.

The Sunset

The burnt orange hue of the sun,
Seeped across the sky
Like watercolours on a canvas,
Slowly the rich orange
Dripped towards the aqua blue sea,
Merging at the horizon,
The canary-coloured sand on the beach,
Changed to a crimson peach.
A solitary, swaying palm tree,
Became tinged with copper,
While the mountains in the distance
Had been painted apricot,
And a stork searching for fish glowed mandarin,
Its body held by legs wire thin.

Dawn

Gradually ebony vanished,
And a thick, grey mist was born,
It dyed the sky a charcoal grey
As if there had just been a storm,
And the flats opposite the park,
Were dirtied to a muddy grey.
The scene looked like a painting depicting Winter
Murky and dark,
But a golden hue had started to lighten the sky
Until out peeped a blessed, yellow ball,
Nature's provider,
Showering the trees with a dazzling light.
The park's pond glimmered and the green grass shimmered,
A truly delightful sight.

Wishful Thinking

I'd like to visit the pyramids of Egypt,
I'd like to go to Niagara Falls,
I'd like to sip champagne in a gondola,
And I'd like to visit the Wailing Wall.
I'd like to visit the Grand Canyon,
I'd like to visit Athens and Rome,
I'd like to see all the shows on Broadway,
And visit the Millennium Dome.
I'd like to gamble in Monte Carlo,
Shop at the salons of Milan,
Go on a round the world cruise,
And to Paris to see the Can-Can.
I'd like to ride on the Orient Express,
See the Hanging Gardens Of Babylon,
Ride a horse by the Swiss Alps,
And visit the city of Bonn.
I'd like to cycle by the Rockies,
Water ski in the south of France,
Swim in the Atlantic and Pacific,
Then in a café in Brazil do Latin dance.
I'd like to go walking in Austria,
Visit New England in the fall,
Go on safari to Kenya,
And dance at The Ritz at a ball.
Instead, I'm stuck in a small flat,
The rain beats on the window-pane,
My mind wanders off again,
And I imagine myself on a beach in Spain.

Far Away

I look at my watch, it says five,
The sun still shimmers on the sea,
I sit at ease on the golden beach,
The breeze blows around my face,
I am glad to be alive and here
Instead of glued in the grey,
Waiting for a bus, tube or train,
To take me through the polluted city,
To live another boring day.

I sip a glass of orange juice,
And watch people swimming in the sea,
Then lie back on my towel,
Breathing slowly and deeply,
Inhaling the clean air.

How could I have lived in a city?
Grit blew from the cracked paving stones,
Cars expelled fumes into the air,
But now I have so much energy
As I am surrounded by beauty,
Instead of derelict warehouses.

I am free to go for long walks,
Or to cycle or read all day,
Instead of being squashed in a train,
Rushing to work for nine,
Not returning home until eight,
Now I have flown far and free,
To the lands of mountains, sand and sea.

Degeneration

Grim, grey, a blanket of filth
Has enshrouded this town,
It has been doomed with gloom,
And the nuclear bomb has dropped,
As all around it is deserted,
Derelict buildings blackened with soot,
Are waiting to be bulldozed down,
No flowers or shrubs can bloom,
In their place are pavements of grit,
And flies eating dog shit.

Bleak, barren, a spider's web has entrapped me,
The threads stick to my skin,
Encircle my body and paralyse me,
I cannot break free, weak with apathy,
Stagnation floods my body,
Poisoning my blood, turning it black,
My brain is being drained of intellect,
Words no longer flow from my pen,
But tears stream from my eyes,
Because I don't have wings to fly.

Grim, grey, a blanket of filth
Has enshrouded this town,
Bleak, barren, a spider's web has entrapped me,
The threads stick to my skin,
And I know I won't survive,
Dismal, dreadful, the place is a sewer,
People have fallen in the cesspit,
While inside I wither in the web,
Food for vultures as I become rotting flesh.

The Body

Anorexic

Four stone at five foot ten,
There my sister stands, a skeleton,
But what you see is the girl you were
A girl with bigger hips and thighs
You see her now, instead, and cry.

Your eyes are huge hollows,
Your cheeks sucked away,
All that's left of your face
Is skin stretched over bones.
Your neck is a cocktail stick
Which looks as if it will break
From the weight of your bony head.

Your skin is like tracing paper
Exposing all your ribs and bones
Which protrude like painful lesions;
You're now too small for size eight clothes,
But all you see is fat:
Somebody who has tree trunk arms
And jelly legs.
This is far from the fact.

You look at the models in *Vogue*,
You glance at a poster of Kate Moss,
A tear trickles down your face,
"Oh why can't I be like you," I hear you say,
"I'm so fat, I look terrible,
If I lose weight I'd look great."

I bring a plate of food to you,
You start to cry as you don't want to eat,
"Food will make me fat!" you scream.
"Not if eaten sensibly," I reply.
"Better to eat than to die."

Varicose Veins

Knotted green rivers which spread like a disease,
Disfiguring like fire wherever they appear,
Lumpy and bumpy they stick through the skin,
And my mother smothers them
With support tights because they won't clear.
Some people have surgery because they fear
They'll worsen and destroy their legs,
However these monsters cannot be appeased
As they can breed although
The operation succeeds.
Not immediately, of course, but some years later
Distressing and oppressing by their very nature,
They are encouraged to procreate by
The onset of pregnancy or overweight,
However with some people it's been their fate
To be cursed with these creatures
Because of what their genes dictate;
Jobs too are to blame
Because if you're standing all day,
They'll appear like a fungus
And make you feel ashamed so
That you'll hide your legs
With trousers or long skirts.
What was your prize you can no longer abide
Because of the veins' size,
Surgery, cream and tights don't frighten them,
They cannot be easily killed,
They like to cause harm,
They like to cause alarm
Because they are a plague!

Bust

A pair of balloons sitting on her chest,
Soft, round and moulded by her bra,
They pop through her low-cut tops,
And make men stare,
Whatever she wears, her bust is the star,
They have emboldened her,
Enabling her to go far.

She has appeared in many magazines,
Topless, with just a gold chain around her neck.
They are luscious, plump and firm,
Nipples like little rocks.
They have empowered her,
Enabling her to be free
To live the life she wishes,
Thanks to the money she earns from their display,
No matter what the naysayers may say,
It's her boulders that have made her rich.

Society is obsessed with a woman's bust,
A whole industry caters for this,
Those with melons have been given power
Although not always aware,
Those with peaches feel life's been unfair
But joy can turn to sour cream
When the dream goes wrong—
A woman is more than a pair of breasts,
A woman is more than a proud chest.

Drooping Melons

They are as heavy as cannon-balls,
As soft as marshmallows,
As round as the sun,
And as big as my head,
They droop to my belly button,
They almost break my shoulders
Because they are huge boulders;
The cups of my bra are the size of dinner plates,
That's if I can get one to fit,
Which is rarely the case;
Strapless bras don't support me at all,
So I can't wear tops off the shoulders
Or low back dresses or jumpers
Because my breasts would fall,
I can't wear fitted blouses
Because the buttons would pop off,
I can't go swimming because few costumes have cups.
If I jump in the air
They will crash down like rocks,

If I have an operation, my problems will be solved.
My breasts will change from sagging balloons .
To firm, pretty peaches.
I will be able to wear whatever I want.
My shoulders will be pushed back and proud,
And when I look in the mirror I will be too.

Stereotypes

If you're fat you're a clown,
Some people laugh and call you names,
They think you're stupid,
That you eat too much,
That for your size you are to blame.

If you're skinny some people like to attack you,
Because you look weak,
They think you're anorexic,
They laugh when you say you wear a bra,
And they make you feel like a freak.

If you're short even children are rude to you,
Although you might be fifty,
Some people are protective, others are patronising,
Why oh why should this be?

If you're tall you look threatening,
So most people leave you alone,
There are many jobs that value the tall:
Security guard, basketball player and model are just a few,
Your height puts you in a protected zone.

But if you're a size 24 or a size 8,
If you're 6 foot 4 or 4 foot 8,
It's difficult to buy clothes,
Society caters for the average,
It's about time everyone should feel great.

Difference should be valued,
People aren't supposed to be clones,
Individualism needs to remain,
To prevent the world being a banal place.

Pregnancy

My mind is a nail hammered in a plank of wood,
I rise from bed like a zombie,
Then rush into the bathroom to be sick,
Vomit spurts from my mouth like a putrid fountain,
I struggle to wash but all energy has deserted me.

My stomach is already a balloon,
Skirts with zips no longer fit.
I despair as I search in my wardrobe
For something to wear,
My sweaty hands stick to everything I touch.
I can't find anything, so lie down
For the rest of the day.

The thought of food makes me feel ill,
All my favourites have become enemies:
I can't bear burgers, crisps or cake,
Instead I like eating oranges, spinach and steak.
I am restless at night, wanting something to eat,
And finding I have to frequently urinate,
So for much of the night I am awake.

I feel as helpless as an ant,
Not in control of my life,
All I can do is lie down,
With a wet flannel on my forehead.
How is it I can feel life growing inside of me
Yet feel my own is ebbing away from me?

Chocolate

You are a devil,
You are an angel,
You'll be my death,
Or my salvation,
You bring me happiness,
Cut through with shame,
As you increase my weight,
So my clothes no longer fit.

I feel myself transported
To Paradise when I eat you,
But when you've been digested,
I'm brought back to reality:
I have a pile of ironing to do
Which I don't think I'll get through today.
The baby cries, the toddler yells,
I look in the cupboard for you,
But you're not there.
I have a cup of coffee
But it's a poor substitute,
Oh, to have you back,
My guilty pleasure,
My cherished treasure.

The Past

Colonialism

The monster lurches over the begging dog
Across the Irish Sea,
Imposing its evil ideology
Of subordination and slavery.

The monster encroached on Scotland and Wales,
Spitting destruction everywhere,
Killing kings and slaughtering the innocent.

The monster bellowed and the world became pink,
It now wore a crown where The Union Jack was put down,
It sneered and snatched,
Becoming rich from greed,
While the tortured were left in poverty,
If they didn't die of disease.

The monster created one of the richest economies,
While people perished, and died like flies
In the exploited colonies,
That Union Jack ransacked.
But it's about time, monster, you gave back,
To all those countries drained of wealth,
Which nurtured your health!

You term these places 'third world,'
But contrary to what you believe,
They were advanced societies
Before you appeared with your guns and your missionaries,
Your shackles and inhumanity.
Your Sterling is stained with blood,
From centuries of cruelty,
Reparations should be given to these pillaged lands,
Which put millions into your evil hands.

Slavery

Your face wears years of torture,
Picking cotton on the plantation
For not even a dollar a day,
Your back is covered with scars
From the lashes of the overseer's whip
Because he thought you were lazy.
Your child was taken from you
At the age of two to a place far away.
It has been ten long years
And you haven't seen him since.
Your lover was sold eight years ago
To a planter in Virginia.
He might as well be dead,
As you'll never see him again

I wish there was something I could have done,
But I didn't live then,
All I can hope is that the same thing
Doesn't happen again,
Otherwise the world should be destroyed.

The master and mistress hold lavish balls
And dress in bright silk and satin
While you only have a dull cotton dress.
They eat large plates of food
While you only have scraps.
They belch and laugh,
Your stomach groans as you lie alone
In a tiny, dark shack.
They dance merrily as the music plays,
While silent tears stream down your face:
You think of your child and your lover.
They drink lots of wine,

While you have only your tears.
The master and mistress kiss with passion,
While there are screams from nearby
As the overseer gets his way
With another helpless slave.

I wish there was something I could have done,
But I didn't live then.
All I can hope is that the same thing
Doesn't happen again,
Otherwise the world should be destroyed.

I close the book as I can read no more,
I close the book as I can no longer
Look at those pictures which denote such pain,
I am filled with sorrow,
Because while so many suffered from slavery,
Others gained and became extremely wealthy.

Legacy of Empire

Rule Britannia, Britannia rules the waves,
This is no longer the case,
The empire has withered and died,
But her principles remain alive,
Of imposing her ideology,
And sneering at other people,
Slaughtering their laws and customs,
So that none of their beliefs survive;
Christianity was a tool,
To make them into docile fools,
On the syllabus was English history,
To make them lack an identity,
The greatness of Shakespeare was revered,
While national writers were sneered at,
Even the blonde wig was worn
To signify the dawn of Western thought,
But it's been a tragedy for the conquered,
As Britannia, like a locust,
Has ravaged everywhere,
Excreting poverty, famine, death and despair,
Sucking all the resources,
Forcing countries into world debt.
Colonies no longer exist,
But the Crown heads the Commonwealth Table,
Talking triviality while more people die,
Because they can't survive
In the Empire which is very much alive.
Now charity workers are sent
Who try to prevent the suffering,
But if Britannia really cared,
She'd cancel the debt,

Allow people to trade and pay
Them a decent wage,
Rather than cause dismay.
Britannia's greed will continue to lead
To further hardship and poverty,
She will continue to get fat,
While her human possessions remain in need!

The Glorious Twenties

The 1920s was a time of fun,
Parties, dancing, gambling, gangsters and the gun,
Jazz, boot-legging, sequins, feathers and the crash,
Bobs, liberation, strikes, starvation and hash!
People getting rich, people becoming poor,
Living is a party, living is a chore;
The "Model T" was symbolic of wealth,
While slums slaughtered poor people's health;
People laughing at a silent movie,
People begging for a cup of tea,
Miners underpaid, judges overpaid,
Factory tyrants making the workers afraid;
Noel Coward plays depicted a life of bliss,
Bright Young Things were granted many a wish,
Wodehouse and Priestly were the world above stairs,
Pubs and music halls were the servants' cares,
Fear of Communism in the USA,
Bans on immigration swelling every day,
Men in white robes holding the burning cross,
Lynching, looting, mocking the Negro's loss,
Catholicism scorned, Judaism attacked,
Al Jolson and others their faces blacked;
Vaudeville and Gershwin people adored,
The public filled the theatres
And were never bored,
Valentino and Swanson, the gods of the day,
Had so many pennies which they threw away,
Flappers giggling, wiggling and puffing away,
In a world where justice reigned everyday:
Al Capone, Versailles, Weimar and Mosley;
Hatred and greed was a ferocious sea,

The wave of Nazism was roaring to the shore,
People were becoming greedier for more,
Discontent was rising as want was thriving,
Some were squandering, others surviving,
Suicide was rife when the stock market crashed,
And the glorious twenties lifestyle was dashed.

The 1960s

The Beatles, Bob Dylan and The Rolling Stones,
"Flower Power," LSD and free love,
The Pill, the legalisation of abortion and homosexuality,
The Profumo Affair in 1963,
Freed from stockings, women wore tights
And skirts so short their parents found it shocking,
A rocket zoomed into the sky,
And the first man landed on the moon,
While on earth people raced around in their Mini cars,
And the TV gave birth to "kitchen sink" stars,
Race riots in The States and the Vietnam War,
The dawn of a new age was born with welfare reform, introduced by JFK,
But he was shot, as was Dr King,
Still, civil rights emerged in America,
Whereas in England there were notices which said:
"No blacks, no Irish, no dogs,"
And many used words like "paddy" and "wog",
The Conservative election campaign stated:
"If you want a nigger for a neighbour vote Labour,"
Enoch Powell gave his "Rivers Of Blood" speech,
And he was elected MP for Wolverhampton South West;
Marilyn, siren of the silver screen, was found dead,
And her death remains a mystery,
The currency in England was pounds, shillings and pence,
The country proposed an unpopular policy on defence,
There were CND marches and many arrests,
Mary Whitehouse protested about indecency
And violence in television and film,
Macmillan, Douglas-Home and Wilson were Prime Ministers
In a decade that was the firework which ignited change.

The 1970s

Platform shoes, long hair and flares,
Tank tops, maxi skirts and bright shirts,
Slade, Sweet and T-Rex topped the charts,
As well as the Carpenters, Mud and Gary Glitter.
People didn't seem to have a care,
But then there was the three day week,
Britain joined the EEC,
Some felt this shouldn't be
The path that the country followed;
Decimilisation changed the currency,
Heath clashed with the miners and they went on strike,
Bombs were exploding in Northern Ireland,
And the USA was still in Vietnam,
Wanting her to become like Uncle Sam,
Nixon was disgraced by Watergate,
Was replaced by Gerald Ford,
And the Cold War was abated by Détente.
"Love Story" was on at the cinema,
"New Faces" made unknowns into stars,
And Shaft was a TV hero.
Muhammad Ali won many fights,
And talked on Parkinson about The Nation Of Islam,
At the Munich Olympics some Israelis were shot dead,
But the games continued nevertheless
Although the Israeli tragedy was publicised greatly
By television news and the press;
Arthur Ash was the first Black player
To win Wimbledon in 1975,
Borg dominated the game in the mid and late '70s,
While Olga was the prodigy of gymnastics,
Her performance was filled with so much drive;

The Beetle was in vogue and so was the Chopper bike,
And then there was a craze for the skateboard,
Which some parents couldn't afford to buy their children;
Punk blasted like a rocket onto the scene,
Spiked hair and piercings became the fashion,
And punks appeared on TV who didn't sing but screamed,
Some felt that they were really obscene;
There was the Silver Jubilee
When many held street parties,
But this time of glee was ended
By the Winter Of Discontent,
And Thatcher and the decade of greed was on the horizon.

Thank You Mrs Thatcher

You came to reign after the Winter of Discontent,
And the seeds of despair were sown into boom years,
But along with the honeymoon there was gloom.

Yuppies talking on mobile phones,
Making millions at the city,
But nearby stood derelict estates,
And although tenants had "the right to buy,"
Many couldn't afford to own their home,
And those on the council waiting list increased
While you decreased grants
For the building of property.

You abolished the GLC and ILEA,
Increased fares on the Tube,
The miners went on strike
And there were industrial disputes.
The Falklands War just after
The explosion on the streets
In Brixton, Toxteth and Moss Side,
Because many couldn't abide police brutality.
Unemployment soared and so did crime,
And many rebelled against the Poll Tax
At Trafalgar Square,
But you didn't care that you caused despair.

Thank you Mrs Thatcher for being
Prime Minister for just over a decade,
You may be a Baroness,
But we'll remember you best
As The Iron Lady.